Splash into Safe Swimming

by Susie Heinzelman

Illustrated by Rebecca Hirsch

To the thousands of children who have learned to swim with me.

Hopefully, I have started a perseverance of saving lives that will go on forever.

Do

Smile and be happy.
Wear sunscreen.
Swimming can be
lots of fun!

Do Not

Run around a pool.
Dive from a deck, only
from a diving board.
Go potty in my pool.
Every night, I get my
"Magic Crystals" and I
put them in the pool!
Wear googles when
learning how to swim.

Water is Everywhere

Oceans
Lakes
Ponds

Streams
Rivers
Gorges

Good morning to all my friends.

Please open your ears to listen to your teacher.
Please open your eyes to watch your teacher.
Please remember to use my bathroom.
Please try your best during your lessons.
Please let me see your beautiful smiles.

Mother or Daddy Duck, please have the ducklings walk down the steps into the pool. Hold onto the sides if you wish or just get used to how the water feels to you. Some of you might even want to try a tube too.

Some of you did it . . . **Yeah for you!**
Everyone try really hard to get your face or your whole head wet.

You all look like jack-in-the-boxes.
"We all go down under . . . and
pop up!"

Let's hold hands with our
new friends and make a giant circle.
Now we will sing "Ring Around the Rosie,"
And when we sing, "Ashes, ashes, we all fall down,"
your whole head should be under the water.
Great job, everyone!

In a few more lessons, we will
try to be synchronized Olympian
swimmers as we attempt to
make a gorgeous flower.

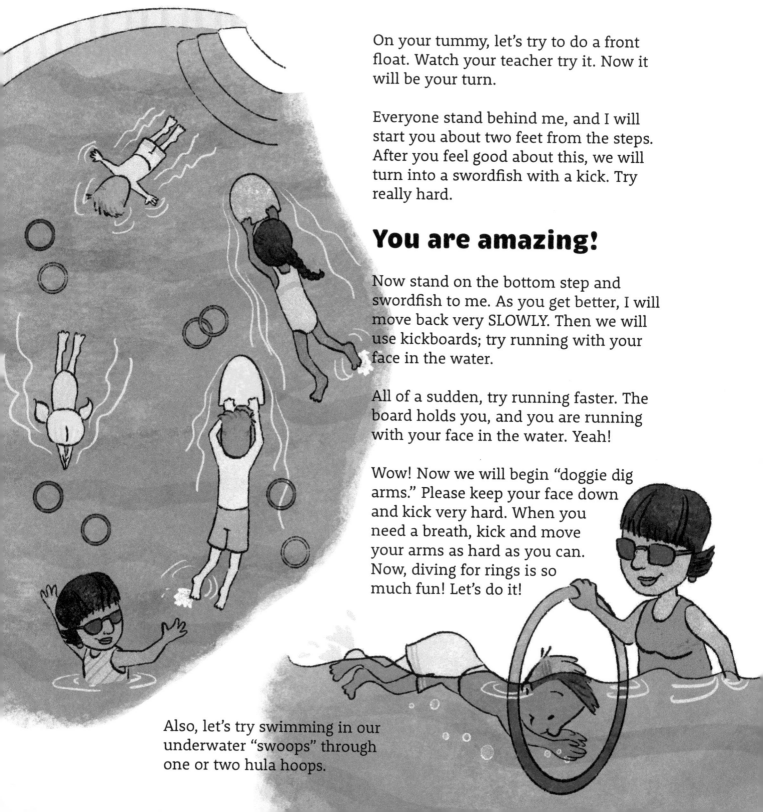

On your tummy, let's try to do a front float. Watch your teacher try it. Now it will be your turn.

Everyone stand behind me, and I will start you about two feet from the steps. After you feel good about this, we will turn into a swordfish with a kick. Try really hard.

You are amazing!

Now stand on the bottom step and swordfish to me. As you get better, I will move back very SLOWLY. Then we will use kickboards; try running with your face in the water.

All of a sudden, try running faster. The board holds you, and you are running with your face in the water. Yeah!

Wow! Now we will begin "doggie dig arms." Please keep your face down and kick very hard. When you need a breath, kick and move your arms as hard as you can. Now, diving for rings is so much fun! Let's do it!

Also, let's try swimming in our underwater "swoops" through one or two hula hoops.

Just by looking at your sweet faces, I can see that you are so excited.

We will now try to do some back floats and the back fin.

I will pass out many colored noodles. Children use noodles to balance on their backs with their hands on the water. Be certain you have the noodle under your arms.

I will count to 20 several times.

Now, let's try kickboards.

You are so good!

It's time to try back floating without much assistance. I will hold your head.

My hand is directly under your head . . . I promise not to move it. Look up at my sunglasses.

WOW! You did it!

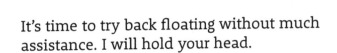

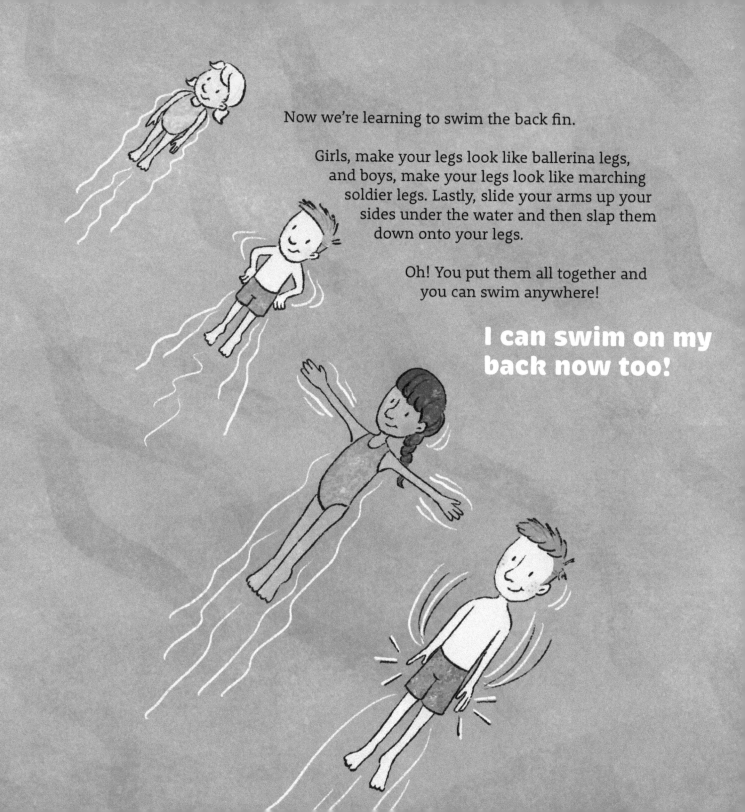

Now we're learning to swim the back fin.

Girls, make your legs look like ballerina legs, and boys, make your legs look like marching soldier legs. Lastly, slide your arms up your sides under the water and then slap them down onto your legs.

Oh! You put them all together and you can swim anywhere!

I can swim on my back now too!

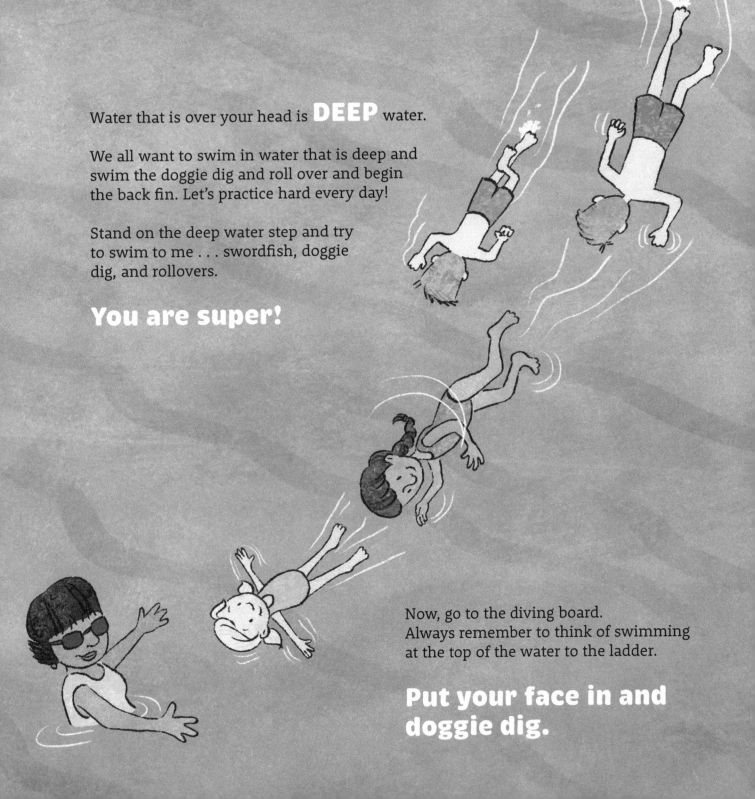

Water that is over your head is **DEEP** water.

We all want to swim in water that is deep and swim the doggie dig and roll over and begin the back fin. Let's practice hard every day!

Stand on the deep water step and try to swim to me . . . swordfish, doggie dig, and rollovers.

You are super!

Now, go to the diving board.
Always remember to think of swimming at the top of the water to the ladder.

Put your face in and doggie dig.

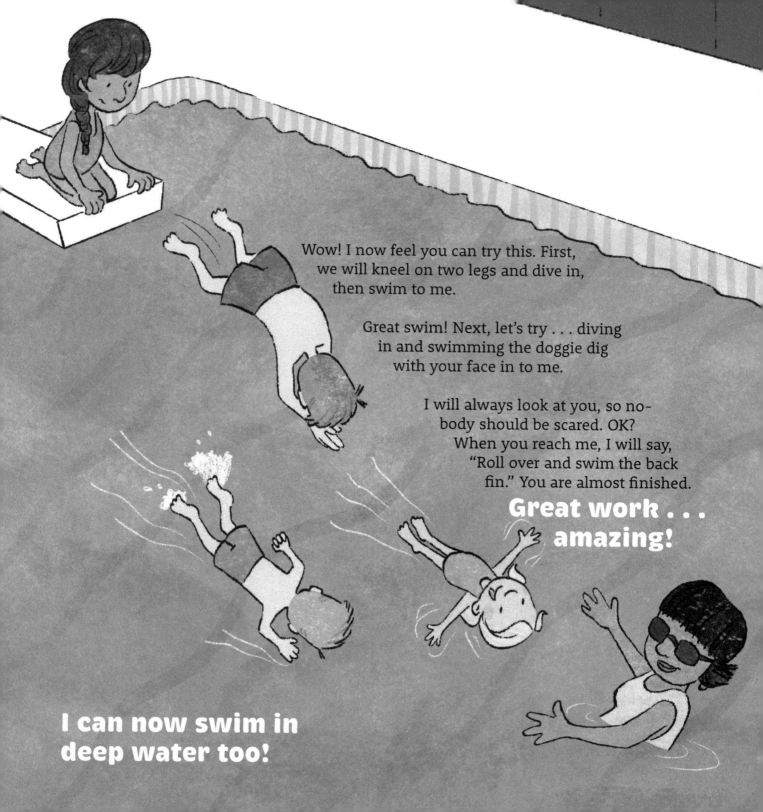

Wow! I now feel you can try this. First, we will kneel on two legs and dive in, then swim to me.

Great swim! Next, let's try . . . diving in and swimming the doggie dig with your face in to me.

I will always look at you, so nobody should be scared. OK? When you reach me, I will say, "Roll over and swim the back fin." You are almost finished.

Great work . . . amazing!

I can now swim in deep water too!

Who can answer this question? What are the three common names for the crawl?
(1) American (2) Front Crawl (3) Freestyle

When learning to properly swim the front crawl, it is very important to walk on the bottom, put your face in the water, and choose your favorite side. Now, bring your one arm out of the water, your elbow up, and reach high up into the sky and stretch forward. While you are stretching, you will do the same with your other arm.

Rhythmic Breathing
Start with a front float. Turn your head to the right or left and pretend you are licking an ice cream cone on your shoulder. Reach your right arm down and elbow up, and then stretch your arm out. Now try your other arm. Very good! This is when you blow your bubbles out (use your nose or your mouth) and only turn to get a new breath on the side you have chosen. Please try your "fast" flutter kick.

You are amazing at this!

See me try the front crawl! Outstanding!

The next tricks that I know you can do are the front and back floats, jellyfish (survival stroke), bobs, and now it is time to **tread water.**

Watch your teacher.
Sit on the bike seat and ride your bike with your legs and feet.
Now slide and slap your legs.

Wow, you are the best!

You know how to swim the front crawl, so now let's learn the back crawl and the elementary backstroke.

Back Crawl

Lie on your back, start kicking a "flutter kick," raise one arm and push it way up into the sky over your head. Now do the same with the other arm. Point your fingers, straight arms up just like a pinwheel.

You are so good at this!

Back Crawl

Your arms and legs do this:

Chicken

Eagle

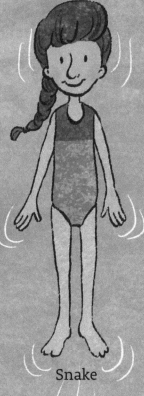

Snake

I can now swim on my back three ways: back fin, back crawl, and elementary backstroke.

Elementary Backstroke

This is a very fun stroke. You can be a chicken, an eagle, and a snake— one after the other. Remember to float for three seconds.

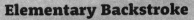

Sidestroke

The sidestroke is fun and easy. I always say this is Grandma's favorite stroke. She loves it because she never gets her hair wet. Lie on your favorite side with your arm raised on top of the water. Now put your head on your arm. Your other arm rests on your hip. Walk across the pool by reaching for the apple high on the water. Now bring it down, and the hand that's on your hip moves up to get the apple and put it back into the original position (into a basket). Remember, please keep your head on your upper arm at all times.

Leg Practice

Lift both legs into a jellyfish position. Then pretend you are spreading these legs into a scissors position. Now snap the legs back into the original position.

Put your arms and legs together for the sidestroke. All actions are moving at the same time. Grandma loves this part—the three-second glide. She feels like she is just zooming across the water.

Oh! Grandma, now I know how to swim your favorite stroke!

Finally, the breaststroke is our last stroke to learn.
Think of "Little Robin Red Breast." Her tummy is red, so
put your tummy down and your face in the water. We
will start by using a front float position. Now lift
your head up and make one small pizza with your
arms and a large pizza with your legs, pointing
all toes away from your body. Now front
float again. This is your glide position
for three seconds. Similar to the front
crawl, now watch your hands make
the small pizza while your legs do
the same. Once again, be in a
front float position to blow out
your bubbles into the water.
Then repeat by lifting
your head, two pizzas,
front float, and glide
for three seconds.

Finally, I can swim the breaststroke. It is hard, but
after lots of practice, I now feel very happy.

Congratulations to all!

I'm so very happy you have enjoyed my book SPLASH INTO SAFE SWIMMING. However, before you close, please read through these most important safety skills that you might want to share with your friends and family.

Water Capitals

In many areas of our country, we have "water capitals." These have many water slides. Never go down a slide if you are not good at deep-water swimming. Be certain your parent or an adult is on the bottom to catch you.

Hiking

Many scout troops and other camps throughout our country enjoy various outdoor hiking activities. Be careful. You could slip and fall into an unknown gorge or canyon.

DEEP-WATER Accident

Please remember to DISROBE in this order: shoes, socks, sweatshirts, pants.
Then use the five safety skills:
- **front float**
- **back float**
- **tread water**
- **survival float**
- **bob**

Boating and Fishing

Wear a life preserver. Never stand in a small rowboat, sailboat, kayak, or canoe. Fish only by sitting in a small boat or standing in a large boat. Canoes and kayaks are primarily for boating, not fishing.

Published by Orange Hat Publishing 2022
ISBN 9781645383642

www.orangehatpublishing.com

CPSIA information can be obtained
at www.ICGtesting.com
Printed in the USA
BVHW021300190722
642474BV00007B/462

9 781645 383642